T0157263

YES, I CAN.

YOUR GUIDE TO JUNIOR HIGH SCHOOL ACADEMIC SUCCESS.

DAVID S. KYERE

authorHOUSE

AuthorHouse™
1663 Liberty Drive
Bloomington, IN 47403
www.authorhouse.com
Phone: 833-262-8899

Published by AuthorHouse 10/19/2021

ISBN: 978-1-6655-3890-9 (sc)
ISBN: 978-1-6655-3891-6 (e)

Print information available on the last page.

CONTENTS

DEDICATIONS

I dedicate this book to my parents **Anthony Kwaku Kyere** and **Agnes Abena Kyere**, in Asokore-Koforidua, Ghana–West Africa, for their love and care for me all my life, and for their support for me through my educational career with their finances and resources.

I also dedicate this book to my lovely wife **Mrs. Ama Kesewa Kyere**, a paraprofessional of the New York City Department of Education, USA. God bless you for loving and being a blessing to me and my ministry.

I also dedicate this book to my son, **Joshua Nkunim Quaye Kyere**. We love you, son, and pray you grow up to become a great academician.

Finally, I dedicate this book to all **junior high school students** in the world.

THE PROBLEM

Parents around the world are so much concerned about how well their children will do in school, academically, and through life in general. Students all over the world are doing their best to succeed in school but are met with challenges. The author, David S. Kyere, identifies three major causes why students are not doing well academically. The author identifies these causes as:

1. **Lack of time management principles**
2. **Lack of study skills on the part of students**
3. **Lack of planning and organization**

Based on the author's experience in education and working with students for over twenty years, he provides workable and practical solutions in detail in his book *Yes, I Can: Your Guide to Junior High School Academic Success.*

Finally, the author gives general advice to students on a number of social issues that affect them. Although he is not an expert in these matters, the advice will go a long way to help students make better choices in life and minimize negative outcomes in their academics.

WORDS OF WISDOM ABOUT EDUCATION

You can't let your failures define you. You have to let your failures teach you. You have to let them show you what to do differently the next time.

—President Barack Obama

For me, education was power … Through my education, I didn't just develop skills, I didn't just develop the ability to learn, but I developed confidence … You have to stay in school. You have to. You have to go to college. You have to get your degree. Because the one thing people can't take away from you is your education. And it is worth the investment.

—Michelle Obama

The function of education is to teach one to think intensively and to think critically. Intelligence plus character—that is the goal of true education.

—Martin Luther King Jr.

Education promotes equality and lifts people out of poverty. It teaches children how to become good citizens. Education is not just for a privileged few, it is for everyone. It is a fundamental human right.

—Ban Ki-moon

FOREWORD

Professor Gene Adams

Junior high school is weird. Through the years, rapid and monumental changes have taken place in the technology, curriculum design, and even physical design of junior high school buildings. However, the experience of being a junior high schooler remains one of the most awkward phases of a person's life. Simply weird. Now more than ever, parents and educators must make a greater effort to understand what is happening to kids in junior high school. If we try for a moment to remember and connect with our junior high school selves, most of us might shudder from the memory of an embarrassing or awkward experience. Things change during junior high school. Relationships with parents become unexplainably strained, bullying is pervasive, friendships define our sense of meaning, and our bodies and emotions soar in all directions. In this instability and strangeness, kids try and are expected to learn and excel.

Today, in an era dominated by first computer technology and now COVID-19 inspired, ramped-up online models, middle school children desperately need adult empathy, support, and guidance. *Yes, I Can: Your Guide to Junior High School Academic Success* could not have been published at a more critical time. David S. Kyere has spent over a decade teaching, guiding, and inspiring junior high school students in New York City. In his 2010 book, *Yes I Can: Guidelines for Studies for High School Students*, Kyere echoed the popular inspirational phase of then-President Barack Obama. He thoughtfully provided teenage students with advice for excelling, completing, and surpassing high school. Now, after more than ten years working with junior high school students in private and public schools, Kyere has returned with considerable insight on what is happening in junior high school and what tools students need for success.

In *Yes, I Can: Your Guide to Junior High School Academic Success*, Kyere has provided a step-by-step roadmap that parents and teachers can use with students to help them excel through the awkward days of junior high school. Kyere understands that habits stand above talents in the learning matrix. His book offers practical and easy to follow instructions for developing strong study discipline and habits. The ten chapters can be divided to represent two sections.

Chapters I–V focuses on core personal skills that students must master to lay the foundation for sustainable academic achievement. How students experience and view time in respect to learning is key. Time management and respect for process strengthens perspective and personal expectation. Kyere uses planning as the cornerstone for the building blocks of success. Personal discipline provides students with a sense of self awareness and self-worth in why and how they learn.

Chapters IV–X guides and encourages students to assume primary responsibility for their own learning. Students are taught to develop their own study methods, employing creativity and visualization. Kyere gives students insight into how important their own decision making and choices are in their learning and success. One of the most critical areas challenging junior high school students is their lack of awareness around emotional, physical, and mental health. Kyere doesn't shy away from the importance of good health on motivation and wellbeing in learning.

David Kyere has produced a remarkable book that is not only a guide for junior high school students, it is also a tool for parents who understand their role in their child's learning experience. *Yes, I Can: Your Guide to Junior High School Academic Success* is meant to be used by students, parents, and teachers collectively as they navigate and excel through the learning and developmental challenges of junior high school.

INTRODUCTION

"Yes, we can!" is a rallying cry popularized by Barack Obama when he campaigned to become the 44th President of the United States of America. When Obama was elected on November 4, 2008, he gave a victory speech at Grant Park in Chicago in which he assured a crowd of nearly 250,000 people, and tens of millions more watching via TV and the internet, that we can do anything we set our minds to.

Referring to a citizen who voted at age 106, he said, "Tonight, I think about all that she's seen throughout her century in America—the heartache and the hope; the struggle and the progress; the times we were told that we can't; and the people who pressed on with that American creed: 'Yes, we can!'"

With this theme as its guiding principle, this book sets a detailed and practical guide of how students all over the world can manage their time, study effectively, practice self-care, and find their true selves.

By building their skills and confidence, it will help students balance their academic work with their personal lives and do their very best academically. It will also guide students and young individuals to develop the right habits for a highly successful future career. After reading this book, a student will be able to confidently and boldly proclaim, "Yes, I can!"

CHAPTER 1

WHY TIME MANAGEMENT IS IMPORTANT

Poor time management is one of the main issues most people, especially middle-school students, struggle with. This often creates frustration when they don't get things accomplished. Students often procrastinate, lack time-management skills, or waste time. This attitude concerning time has a tremendous impact on students' academic work. There are a number of published research works that have shown a strong correlation between time management and academic performance. In this chapter, I discuss why time management is important and provide practical steps and solutions for students.

Your life largely consists of what you do with your time. So, making the best use of your time means living your most productive and fulfilling life.

In fact, many students succeed or fail academically as a result of how well or poorly they manage their study and homework schedules.

As a result, the first half of this book will help you organize and maximize your time to ensure you balance your studies and other schoolwork with your personal activities. This will allow you to consistently complete everything you need to do day after day.

Investing in Your Time

One of your most important resources is your time. Like money, your time is finite and precious—and you should take care to spend it wisely.

For example, if you have three hours available to do a homework assignment, and you can actually complete it in one hour, don't drag it out. Get it done promptly. Use the remaining two hours to read ahead in your textbooks, put extra effort into studying a subject that you find difficult, or do something else that will help you perform better in school.

Try to match your work with your unique needs. If you're a night person, schedule your studying for the evening. If you're a morning person, consider getting up extra early to do your reading. The more you're feeling at your best, the more likely you are to pay close attention to, fully understand, and remember what's in your textbooks.

Organizing and managing your time takes effort. But it's well worth doing. **Investing in your time is almost certain to improve your academic performance.**

Managing your time is also a valuable habit to develop for your future. It will help you in whatever career you end up choosing.

Avoid Procrastination

Sometimes we put things off because our mind needs time to process information and to come up with the best ways to perform a task.

But more often, we simply don't feel like doing the work involved in focusing, thinking, and studying.

When you procrastinate, it can lead to problems such as the following:

- You waste valuable time that could otherwise be used for learning, or even socializing with friends. In a sense, you're stealing time from yourself and throwing away opportunities to enrich the quality of your life.
- You're creating situations where you have to get your work done quickly, at the last minute. This can cause you to do sloppy work which can be embarrassing. It can also cause your mind to emotionally link doing homework to stress and discomfort—and will make it even harder for you to sit down and work the next day.
- You risk falling seriously behind on your work. The more you fall behind, the more difficult it will be to get caught up—and the more likely you are to avoid the whole situation by procrastinating even more.

- You put pressure on the rest of your schedule, which doesn't account for you wasting large amounts of your work time. This can end up making you late for everything and disrupting your whole life.
- You might develop a habit of procrastinating, which would be terrible for your future career.

To avoid procrastination, consider doing one or more of the following instead:

- If you receive an assignment on Monday that's due on Friday, do your best to get it done by Tuesday or Wednesday. That way you'll spare yourself from having it hanging over your head for the rest of the week. In addition, you can read your work on Thursday with fresh eyes. You may make improvements you otherwise wouldn't have thought of before you hand in your work on Friday.
- If you receive an assignment that's big or intimidating, you might put it off because you're not sure how to even begin. But if you break the assignment down into small, easily doable parts, you can simply tackle it piece by piece. The more you get done, the higher your confidence will rise—and the easier it'll be to complete the whole assignment promptly.
- If you're feeling stuck, lay down for fifteen minutes, or go for a quick walk around the block, while thinking about how to solve whatever the problem is. Then come back refreshed and eager to work.
- Tell yourself that when you waste time, you're damaging the quality of your life. Think about the activities you can treat yourself to after you get caught up on all your work—and then buckle down and do it.

Professionals who successfully complete assignments not only on time but comfortably ahead of schedule are among the most prized in the workplace. So, even beyond your academic performance, if you develop the habit of getting things done as soon as possible, you'll gain a skill that both employers and clients will value for the rest of your life.

Situations beyond Your Control

Sometimes reasons outside of your control, such as illness or family problems, can cause you lose time and fall behind.

Whatever the cause, it's important to make up for the lost time as soon as possible, so you don't fall even further behind.

Ways to get caught up on your studies include the following:

- If you take the bus or taxi to school, study while you're waiting for your transportation to arrive, and study during your commute.
- Study during the time you're waiting for your teacher or classes to start.
- Spend part of your lunch hour studying in your school's library or reading room.
- Find activities in your schedule that are optional, such as playing video games or watching TV, and replace them with study periods.
- Study whenever you're waiting for something, such as your parents coming to pick you up after school.

Of course, you don't have to follow any of the suggestions above if you don't want to. But however you manage it, find ways to make up the lost time as soon as possible. Doing so will spare you from the stress of not being able to catch up with schoolwork and will help make you feel fully in control of your life again.

CHAPTER 2

CREATING YOUR PERSONAL TIMETABLE

One of the most useful tools for organizing and managing your time is a personal timetable. This will help you create a clearly defined schedule, ensuring you have plenty of time for your studies—which in turn will help you perform better academically.

The materials you'll need to make your timetable are simple: an 8.5" x 11" sheet of paper, a ruler, a pencil with eraser, a pen, your daily school schedule ... and anything else you feel will be helpful.

Alternatively, if you're comfortable using an app that works with rows and columns, such as Microsoft Excel or Word, create your timetable with that software program.

Planning Your Timetable

When planning your personal timetable, here are some things to keep in mind:

- Have a clear understanding of what you hope this timetable will do for you.
- For example, your main goal may be to spend more focused time on your studies, so you can do better academically.
- Or your goal may be to have a better balance between studying and your personal life.
- Include whatever is most important to you in how you create your timetable.

- A timetable is a personal tool that's unique to you. So don't copy anyone else's timetable, and don't pay attention to anyone claiming to have a better timetable than yours. No one knows you better than yourself, so carefully and patiently create a schedule that meets your own unique needs and wants.
- Study your school's timetable, because you'll need to plan your personal timetable around it.
- Set your personal timetable within a specific and limited period of time—for example, next week, or next month, or for spring semester.
- If creating your timetable manually, use a pencil for your first try so you can easily make corrections by erasing. Once you've had some practice, you can switch to using a pen.
- Specify the start and stop times for each class or activity; for example, "Social Studies 11:00 a.m.-12:00 p.m." This will make clear the time to start an activity and when you can move on to something else.
- Make sure there are no conflicts between your school schedule and your personal timetable. Give yourself enough time to get from the end of a class to the start of a personal activity.
- You're sure to prefer certain classes and subjects over others, but don't neglect setting aside enough study time for the ones that you find less appealing. To be a good student, you should try to do well in all subjects.
- Include resting periods, snack times, and other breaks on your timetable. This will help you avoid taking unscheduled breaks that end up lasting a long time and interfere with your schedule.
- Plan your schedule when you're in a quiet and calm place. Dealing with noise, talking to friends, and other distractions may keep you from making an effective timetable.
- Don't plan your timetable when you have a major event, such as a big test or a birthday party, happening later that day. You won't be focused, and you might make poor scheduling decisions.
- For each subject, keep in mind whether you usually learn it quickly or need extra time for studying. If it's a subject you easily understand, you can schedule less time for it. But if it's a tougher subject for you, then schedule more time for it—even if it's a topic that doesn't really interest you. Also consider asking your teacher for advice on how to get a better handle on it. Otherwise, you might fall further and further behind on that subject and have a really hard time catching up.

- Be aware of whether you are *diurnal,* meaning you're most comfortable during daylight hours, or *nocturnal,* meaning you prefer the night. Schedule your studying for whatever period of time makes you feel at your best, because that's when you're likely to do your best work.

- Some prefer to study at night, because it's quiet and free of distractions. However, it's also easier to fall asleep at night … which can be a problem if you have a test the next day. So be honest with yourself about what really works best for you.

- Decide whether you study better by yourself or with a group of your classmates. If you study alone, create a schedule that focuses on what's most effective for you. If you study with a group, keep the schedules of everyone else in mind in addition to your own, and leave room on your timetable for group discussions.

- If you want to watch TV, interact on social media, talk on the phone, and so on, reserve time for that on your timetable. However, don't let these personal activities cut into your study time. Once you create your schedule, stick to it.

- Your timetable isn't only a tool for planning the future. It can also serve as a valuable record of your past. Jot down the things you learn each day that you value the most in your timetable. This will help you remember them for a long time, preserve them in case you forget, and even identify the exact day that you learned them. Plus, you can copy the best items to your study guide (see Chapter 6).

Creating Your Timetable

1. Gather an 8½" x 11" sheet of paper, a ruler, a pencil with eraser, a pen, your school timetable, and anything else you might need. Alternatively, if you're comfortable using an app that supports rows and columns, such as Microsoft Excel or Word, use that app to create a timetable comparable to the one described in the following steps.

2. Position your sheet of paper horizontally—that is, wide rather than tall.

3. Use your ruler to draw seven evenly-spaced lines across the width of the sheet to create rows. These rows represent the seven days of the week.

4. Label the top row with the starting date for next week, and label each of the rest of the rows with the day it represents. Start by assigning Monday to the second row, and then Tuesday, Wednesday, Thursday, Friday, Saturday, and Sunday. It'll look something like this:

Day/Time
Monday
Tuesday
Wednesday
Thursday
Friday
Saturday
Sunday

5. Study your school timetable to see how it schedules your class times. Then think about how you can schedule your entire week, taking your classes into account.

6. Keeping in mind what you've thought about in Step 5, decide on the best way to divide your days into time periods, which will be represented by columns on your timetable.

7. When you have made your choices, use your ruler to draw lines from top to bottom. These lines create columns on your timetable representing time periods. For example, if you want to order your day into two-hour time periods, you could use your ruler to divide your sheet into evenly-spaced columns, drawing a line from the top to the bottom of the sheet for each column. It would look something like this:

Day/Time									
Monday									
Tuesday									
Weds.									
Thurs.									
Friday									
Saturday									
Sunday									

8. In the top row, write the time period that each column represents. For example, if you decided to use two-hour time periods, write *9 a.m. –11 a.m.* for the first column, *11 a.m.–1 p.m.* for the second column, *1 p.m.–3 p.m.* for the third column, and so on until you have assigned a two-hour time period to each column. It would look something like this:

Note: This type of template is only good if you have a routine schedule you follow every day with a fixed two-hour period.

Day/ Time	9am -11am	11am -1pm	1pm -3pm	3pm -5pm	5pm- 7pm	7pm -9pm	9 pm -11pm
Monday							
Tuesday							
Weds.							
Thurs.							
Friday							
Saturday							
Sunday							

9. Your sheet now has a grid of rows and columns with each box or cell representing a specific day and time period. This blank timetable will serve as the template for all your future timetables. Make copies of this timetable. For example, if you are creating it on paper, make photocopies of it. Alternatively, if you are creating it using software, save copies of it using names such as "Personal Timetable," and so on.

Below are Sample timetables of two students from different schools whose Monday to Friday schedules are mostly routine. In this case Monday through Friday have similar time intervals. However, their weekend schedules are different and have their own time on top of the days.

David S. Kyere

SAMPLE A

Name of Student: **Praise Nnadiri** Country: **USA** School: **Lakeland Copper School** Class: **Grade 7** Hobby: **Learn Languages, Crocheting** Career Choice: **Don't Know Yet**

Day/ Time	6am-8am	8am-9:30am	9:30am-3:40pm	3:40pm-5pm	5pm-7pm	7pm-8pm	8pm-10:30pm	10:30pm-6am
Mon	Wake up, exercise	Shower & eat breakfast	Classes at school	Homework	Study Japanese	Dinner, reading	Reading & meditation	Go to bed
Tues	Wake up, exercise	Shower & eat breakfast	Classes at school	Homework	Study Japanese	Dinner, reading	Reading & meditation	Go to bed
Wed	Wake up, exercise	Shower & eat breakfast	Classes at school	Homework	Study Japanese	Dinner, reading	Reading & meditation	Go to bed
Thurs	Wake up, exercise	Shower & eat breakfast	Classes at school	Homework	Study Japanese	Dinner, reading	Reading & meditation	Go to bed
Fri	Wake up, exercise	Shower & eat breakfast	Classes at school	Homework	Study Japanese	Dinner, reading	Reading & meditation	Go to bed

	8am-9am	9am-12pm	12pm-2pm	2pm-5pm	5pm-6pm	6pm-9pm	9pm-11pm	11pm-7am
Sat	Wake up, brush teeth	Watch Japanese drama	Time with family	Homework, reading	Crocheting	Dinner, watch television	Study Japanese	Go to bed

	7am-8am	8am-9am	9am-1pm	1pm-4pm	4pm-6pm	6pm-9pm	9pm-11pm	11pm-6am
Sun	Shower & do makeup	Drive to church	Church time	Lunch & time with family	Watch movies	Dinner, homework	Reading Listen to music	Go to bed

SAMPLE B

Name of Student: **Steven Annan** Country: **USA** School: **Harriet Tubman Charter School** Class: **Grade 6** Hobby: **Playing Games** Career Choice: **Teacher**

DAYS/ TIME	6am-7am	7am-3:30pm	3:30pm-5pm	5pm-6:30pm	6:30pm-7pm	7pm-7:15pm	7:15pm-9pm	9pm-6am
Mon	Get ready for school	School time	Afterschool program	Homework	Take a shower	Eat dinner	Watch TV	Sleep
Tues	Get ready for school	School time	Afterschool program	Homework	Take a shower	Eat dinner	Watch TV	Sleep
Wed	Get ready for school	School time	Afterschool program	Homework	Take a shower	Eat dinner	Watch TV	Sleep
Thurs	Get ready for school	School time	Afterschool program	Homework	Take a shower	Eat dinner	Watch TV	Sleep
Fri	Get ready for school	School time	Afterschool program	Homework	Take a shower	Eat dinner	Watch TV	Sleep
	10am-10:15 am	10:15-10:25am	10:25am-11am	11am-2pm	2pm-6pm	6pm-10pm	10pm -10am	
Sat	Brush my teeth	Eat Break-fast	Watch TV	Go to the library	Play games	Work on math	Sleep	
	10am-10:15 am	10:15-10:25am	10:25am-11am	11am-12pm	12pm-3pm	3pm-4pm	4pm-8:30 pm	8:30pm - 6am
Sun	Brush my teeth	Eat Break-fast	Reading	Talk to my friends	Play games on computer	Get ready for church	Go to church	Sleep

In another scenario some students don't have a routine from Monday to Friday but have different times of activities. This template, unlike the others, has different times for each day of the week and looks like this.

Day/Time	9am -11am	11am-1pm	1pm -3pm	3pm-5pm	5pm-7pm	7pm-9pm
Monday						
	5am - 7am	7- 8:30am	8:30-3pm	3pm-6pm	6pm-9pm	9pm-11pm
Tuesday						
	6am-8am	8am-4pm	4pm-5pm	5pm-8pm	8-10pm	10-12am
Weds.						
	6am-7am	7am- 3pm	3pm-6pm	6pm-7pm	7pm-10pm	10-11pm
Thurs.						
	6am-8am	8am- 3pm	3pm-4pm	4pm-6pm	6pm-9pm	9pm-10pm
Friday						
	5am-6am	6am-12pm	12-4pm	4pm-8pm	8pm-9pm	9pm-12am
Saturday						
	8am-9am	9am-2pm	2pm-4pm	4pm-7pm	7pm-10pm	10-11pm
Sunday						

Below are sample timetables of three students from different schools whose Monday to Sunday have different times of activities. In this case, Monday through Friday has different intervals.

SAMPLE C

Name of Student: **Claudia Kyere** Country: **Ghana** School: **King Jesus** Class: **JHS 3** Hobby: **Music And Volleyball** Career Choice: **Nurse**

Day/ Time	5am-7am	7am-4pm	4pm-5pm	5pm-6pm	6pm-7pm	7pm-9pm	9pm-10pm	10pm-6am
Mon	Prepare for school	School	Eat, bath & relax	Study social studies	Time with family	Reading, homework	Listen to music	Go to bed
	6am-7am	**7am-4pm**	**4pm-5pm**	**5 pm-7pm**	**7pm-8pm**	**8pm-9pm**	**9pm-10pm**	**10pm-5am**
Tues	Prepare for school	School	My mum's Store	Dinner, watch tv	Study math	Reading	Science research	Go to bed
	5am-6am	**6am-7am**	**7am-2pm**	**2pm-5pm**	**5pm-6pm**	**6pm-9pm**	**9pm-10pm**	**10pm- 6am**
Wed	Family devotion	Prepare for school	School	Extra classes	Take a nap	Church service	Home-work	Go to bed
	6am-7am	**7am-4pm**	**4pm-5:30pm**	**5:30pm-6pm**	**6pm-8pm**	**8pm-9pm**	**9pm-10pm**	**10pm-6am**
Thurs	Prepare for school	School	Help mum at store	Dinner	Reading & writing	Study science	Music practice	Go to bed
	5am-6am	**6am-7am**	**7am-2pm**	**2pm-5pm**	**5pm-7pm**	**6pm-8pm**	**8pm-10pm**	**10pm- 8am**
Frid	Family devotion	Prepare for school	School	Extra classes	Visit grand-mother's house	Watch TV with cousins	Reading and listen to music	Go to bed
	8am-9am	**9am-12pm**	**7am-9am 12pm-3pm**	**3pm-6pm**	**6pm-7pm**	**7pm-9pm**	**9pm-10pm**	**10pm-7am**
Sat	Wake up, breakfast	General cleaning	Extra classes	Singing rehearsal	Go to the store	Personal learning ICT	TV program	Go to bed
	7am-8am	**8am-9am**	**8-8:30am 9am-1pm**	**1pm-2pm**	**2pm-5pm**	**5pm-7pm**	**7pm-10pm**	**10pm-5am**
Sun	Wake up water the flowers	Prepare for church	Church service	Grandfather's house	Play with cousins	Dinner and Watch TV	Revise notes	Go to bed

David S. Kyere

SAMPLE D

Name of Student: **Rachelle Asare** Country: **USA** School: **Roxboro Middle School**
Class: **Grade 8** Hobby: **Reading** Career Choice: **Lawyer**

Day/Time	6am-7am	7am -3:30pm	3:30pm-5pm	5pm-6pm	6pm-7pm	7pm-7:15pm	7:15pm - 9pm	9pm-6am
Mon	Shower & breakfast	Go to school for my classes.	Eat lunch	Homework	Talk to my mum	Eat dinner,	Shower, play games,	Sleep
	6am-7am	7am -3:30pm	3:30pm-4pm	4pm-5pm	5pm-7pm	7pm-8pm	8:15pm-10pm	10pm-5am
Tues	Shower & breakfast	Go to school for my classes	Hang out with my siblings	Reading, cook & dinner	Homework	Time with family	Shower, go on my phone, read	Sleep
	5am-7am	7am-3:30pm	3:30pm-5pm	5pm-7pm	5:50pm-6pm	6pm-6:15pm	6:15pm-10pm	10pm-6am
Wed	Shower & breakfast	Go to school for my classes.	Go to library and read	Homework, communicate with teachers	Spend time with Mum	Watch the news	Shower & go on social media	Sleep
	6am-7am	7am-3:30pm	3:30-5:30pm	5:30pm-7pm	7pm-8pm	8pm-6:15pm	6:15pm-10pm	10pm-6am
Thurs	Shower & breakfast	Go to school for my classes.	Hang out with siblings	Homework	Eat dinner, talk to family	Watch TV	Shower & play games.	Sleep
	6am-7am	7am-3:30pm	3:30pm-5 pm	5pm-5:40pm	5:50pm - 6pm	6pm-6:15pm	6:15pm-10pm	10pm-8am
Frid	Wake up, shower & breakfast	Go to school and my classes.	Hangs out with friends	Homework practice violin	Homework, talk to my mom	Eat dinner, talk to family	Shower & reading	Sleep
	6am-7am	7am-3:30pm	3:30pm-5pm	5pm-5:50pm	5:50pm-6pm	6pm-8pm	8pm-10pm	10pm-8am
Sat	Do morning exercise	Wake up & eat breakfast, read, movies	Go to groceries or to the park	Drive to the mall	Arrive at the mall	Eat, shop for clothes at mall, ride carousel	Come home, take a nap, read books.	Sleep
	6am-7am	7am-1pm	1pm-2pm	2pm-3pm	3pm-6pm	6pm-6:15pm	6:15pm-10pm	10pm-8am
Sun	Wake up & do my hair	Church service	Memorize scriptures from Sunday school.	Eat lunch	Have fun, play video games.	Eat a snack, watch movies/shows	Get clothes ready for school Read a book	Sleep

10. You are now ready to create your personalized timetable. So, place your school schedule by your sheet or document and copy each item from it into your own timetable. When you are done, all your classes should appear on the cell on your timetable.

11. When you have decided how to make the most out of the hours remaining to you, fill in the rest of the cells in your personal timetable to plan out the rest of your week or month depending on the goal of each student. (When you plan to sleep, just write *Sleep*.)

Here are some examples of weekday entries for a personal timetable:

SAMPLE E

Name of Student: **Elsa Sowah** Country: **Ghana** School: **Mizpah International School** Class: **JHS 3** Hobby: **Swimming** Career Choice: **Pediatrician**

Example of weekday schedule

- 6 a.m. – 7 a.m. **Take shower**
- 7 a.m. – 8 a.m. **Transportation to school**
- 8 a.m. – 2 p.m. **Classes time**
- 2 p.m. – 4 p.m. **Extra classes**
- 4 p.m. – 5 p.m. **Take a taxi home**
- 5 p.m – 6 p.m. **Take shower and dinner**
- 6 p.m. – 7 p.m. **Watch television**
- 7 p.m. – 9 p.m. **Science homework**
- 9 p.m. – 10:30 p.m. **Listen to music**
- 10:30 p.m. – 6 a.m. **Sleeping time**

SAMPLE F

Name of Student: **Amasha Nethmini Silva** Country: **Sri Lanka**
School: **Seventh Day Adventist** Class: **Grade 8**
Hobby: **Gardening/ Reading** Career Choice: **Teacher**

Example of a Saturday schedule

- 5 a.m. – 6 a.m. **Clean the kitchen**
- 6 a.m – 8 a.m. **Work in the garden**
- 8 a.m. – 9 a.m. **Eat breakfast with family**
- 9 a.m. – 10 a.m. **Feed the poultry**
- 10 a.m. – 1 p.m. **Go to the library and read**
- 1 p.m. – 2 p.m. **lunch with family**
- 2 p.m. – 4 p.m. **Play with friends**
- 4 p.m. – 6 p.m. **Study science**
- 6 p.m. – 7 p.m. **Dinner with family**
- 7 p.m. – 8 p.m. **Story telling time**
- 8 p.m. – 9 p.m. **Watch television**
- 9 p.m. – 10 p.m. **Do English homework**
- 10 p.m. – 5 a.m. **Sleeping time**

SAMPLE G

Name of Student: **Wuruchi Ali** Country: **USA** School: **Academic Leadership** Class: **Grade 7** Hobby: **Drawing** Career Choice: **Lawyer**

Example of a Sunday schedule:

- 7 a.m. – 8 a.m. **Wake up and relax**
- 8 a.m. – 9 a.m. **Go to the Deli Grocery**
- 9 a.m. – 12 p.m. **Church service**
- 12 p.m. – 1 p.m. **Lunch**
- 1 p.m. – 3 p.m. **Science homework**
- 3 p.m. – 4 p.m. **Babysitting**
- 4 p.m. – 6 p.m. **Drawing**
- 5 p.m. – 6 p.m. **Do writing assignment**
- 6 p.m. – 7 p.m. **Dinner/ listen to music**
- 7 p.m. – 8:30 p.m. **Do math**
- 8:30 p.m. – 10 p.m. **Watch my series program**
- 10 p.m. – 6 a.m. **Sleeping time**

Timetable Tips

Because there's a limited amount of space on a sheet of paper, you may sometimes find it difficult to fit an activity into your timetable. One way around this is to make up your own shorthand to use in place of fully spelling out words and phrases.

- Wake up: **WP**
- Breakfast: **BF**
- School: **SCH**
- Science Homework: **SH**
- Reading: **R**
- History and Arts: **HA**
- Bible Study: **B.S**
- Sleep: **S**
- Watch Television: **WTV**
- Group Work: **GW**

There's no right or wrong way to do this, so make up whatever abbreviations are most convenient for you to write and remember.

Another way you can use your custom shorthand is to write a summary of your day's schedule on a slip of paper that you keep in your pocket or tape to the cover of your notebook. You may find it quicker and easier to pull out the slip and refer to it than to retrieve the full sheet of paper.

Once you make your timetable, stick to it. The whole point of creating a timetable is to make a plan and then follow it through.

That said, if you find you guessed wrong about how long certain activities will take, then simply make adjustments on your next week's timetable. Just be sure to never shortchange your homework time and study time.

If you design your timetable well and are disciplined about following it, you'll find it becomes a dependable part of your life—and it's almost certain to help you do better academically.

CHAPTER 3

PLANNING AND GETTING THINGS DONE

A popular saying tells us, "If you fail to plan, you plan to fail."

Planning should be an important part of not just your junior high school experience but the rest of your life. So, the sooner you make it a habit, the better.

Creating your personal timetable was an important step in planning your time, so "Good job!" for getting that done.

But there's more that you can do. This chapter will give you ideas on how to further plan your time.

Planning for Tomorrow

A good time to plan your next day is the period of your evening devoted to studying.

So, at the start of your study period, look at your class schedule and ask yourself questions like these:

- What are the topics I should study before my classes tomorrow?
- Do I have any quizzes or tests tomorrow that I should prepare for?
- Are there any subjects I'm struggling with for which I should devote extra time?
- Is there any subject I'm enjoying so much that I should let myself read ahead of the class assignment, and maybe explore reading about outside of my homework?

You don't have to restrict planning to just evenings though. Jot down any thoughts and ideas about what you need to do whenever they occur to you, and then review them whenever you have the time to act on them.

Creating a To-Do List

One of the most useful organizational tools you can create is a to-do list. This is a list of the tasks you need to accomplish.

You can keep this list in a software notepad on your phone or laptop, and print a fresh copy each day. Or you can write it in a paper notepad that you carry around with you.

When you get a homework /assignment or need to borrow a book from the school library, or promise to do a favor for a classmate, enter each task as an entry on your to-do list. This helps ensure that you don't forget to do the task, and also lets you include details related to the task that you might not otherwise recall.

To create a to-do list, follow these steps:

- Get something to write with. Ideally, it should be a software notepad or physical notepad, but even a sheet of paper will do.
- Study your personal timetable, and write down anything you have scheduled that requires planning.
- For each item, create a to-do list item that will help you perform the preparation you need.
- For example, if you have an English class about the first act of Shakespeare's *Julius Caesar* the next day, then write down that you need to read that first act before going to sleep.
- Keep doing this until you have a complete to-do list of tasks to accomplish.
- Assign a priority number—say, from 1 to 5—to each of your tasks.
- Priority can be a combination of several factors, including how quickly it needs to be done and how important it is to get done.
- Optionally assign each task an estimate of how many minutes you think it'll take to perform.
- You can even assign each task a specific time period—for example, "Read Act 1 of Julius Caesar from 7:00 p.m. to 8:00 p.m."
- Organize your tasks until they're in an order that's most helpful for you.
- For example, you could order them from highest priority to lowest priority.

- Or you could order them from easiest to hardest.
- Or you place them in the order in which you intend to complete them.

Once you're done with your list, you have a group of concrete tasks to perform. This makes clear what it is you need to get done as soon as possible.

If you'd like even more structure, you can take things a step further by setting *daily targets*. These are tasks and mini-tasks that you promise yourself to get done by the end of a particular day, no matter what. You can include these as entries on your to-do list but marked with a *DT* to give them extra prominence. Having daily targets give you a laser focus on what you absolutely need to complete before going to sleep.

For example, assume one of the tasks on your to-do list is, "Do astronomy homework from 6:00 p.m. to 8:00 p.m." A mini-task that you can add as a daily target is, "Memorize the names of all the planets in our solar system, ordered by distance from the sun." (FYI, you can achieve that particular daily target by simply remembering this sentence: "My Very Enthusiastic Mother Just Served Us Noodles!" The first letter of each word represents Mercury, Venus, Earth, Mars, Jupiter, Saturn, Uranus, and Neptune.)

Marking select tasks as daily targets helps ensure that you don't neglect anything you consider vital to accomplish before your day ends.

Using a To-Do List

Once you've created your to-do list, follow these steps to use it:

- Start tackling the tasks on your to-do list.
- After you perform each task, cross it out.
- Often the satisfaction of crossing out a completed task is a reward in itself.
- Do as much as you can.

If you have leftover tasks, hang onto them and schedule time for when you can perform them.

After you stop working but before you go to sleep, evaluate how you did. For example, ask yourself these questions:

- Was I able to accomplish everything I'd planned?
- If not, was I close?

- If not, why not?
- How can I do better next time?

If you get in the habit of carrying your to-do list around with you and recording in it everything you need to do, you're unlikely to forget or neglect to take care of whatever tasks you need to tackle on any given day.

Examples of to-do list:

SAMPLE H

Name of Student: **Hillary Babalola** Country: **USA** School: **Lafayette Academy** Class: **8ᵗʰ Grade** Hobby: **Cooking** Career Choice: **Nurse**

To do list for Monday to Friday (weekdays)

1. Make my bed in the morning
2. Take a shower and brush my teeth
3. Go downstairs to class on zoom
4. Finish my schoolwork
5. Make my siblings food
6. Call with my friends and play
7. Read the Bible
8. Eat dinner and brush my teeth
9. Pray and go to sleep

Note: Once you complete any task, cross it out.

For example, when you complete the assignment "finish my school work," then you cross out point number 4 as shown above.

SAMPLE I

Name of Student: **Ephraim Kwadwo Kyere** Country: **Ghana**
School: **Aspire Educational Complex** Class: **JHS 1** Hobby: **Football, Gaming & Reading** Career Choice: **Scientist**
To do list for Saturday and Sunday (Weekend)

1. Clean the microwave

2. Play video games with friends

3. Do my science homework.

4. Play soccer / football.

5. Visit my cousin.

6. Fly drones with my brother.

7. Go to church.

8. Watch TV with family.

9. Read my books.

CHAPTER 4

BEING DISCIPLINED

There are probably many things you have fun doing. When you're engaged in something pleasurable, such as hanging out with friends, swimming, or playing a video game, it can be difficult to tear yourself away and switch to something you're obligated to do, such as homework or schoolwork.

This is where discipline comes in. Leaving an activity you cherish to take on something that's necessary for your schooling requires a certain amount of determination and will power. But the rewards include attaining academic excellence and being in a stronger position to pursue the long-term goal of an exciting and fulfilling career.

The following are some of the biggest challenges to discipline:

- **Hanging out with friends:** It's great to spend time with friends, whether it's in person, by telephone, or via Skype. But when you're scheduled to do your homework, you have to politely excuse yourself and get your work done. If they're good friends, they'll not only understand but support you.

- **Playing video games:** Interactive games can be great fun, but also addictive. It's fine to schedule time for playing, but then stick to that schedule. You can always return to a game another day.

- **Watching TV:** If there are more shows you want to see than you have time for on a school night, record them and then schedule time to watch them over the weekend. Also resist the temptation to have your TV on in the background. Your studies require your full attention.

- **Cruising the Web and social media:** There's a wealth of information and learning on the Web, and it's fine to schedule time to hang out there. It's

23

also fine to use your computer to help with your homework. But if you find yourself getting distracted by sites that have nothing to do with schoolwork during a time that you've scheduled for studying, force yourself to get back on track and refocus on your homework.

- **Eating after dinner:** If you're in the habit of snacking or eating while you're studying in the evening, try to break it. Eating makes your body focus on digesting and processing the food, which can make you sleepy and less able to focus clearly on your books. It's also not healthy for you to eat shortly before you go to sleep. If you must chew on something, choose a vegetable like carrot, which is easy for your body to digest and won't have an impact on your concentration.

- **Avoiding a subject you don't like:** If there's a school subject you don't like, you may feel tempted to spend most of your time studying the subjects you enjoy and only a little time on the one you don't. That would be a mistake, because the typical reason for not liking a subject is not knowing it well enough to be good at it. The solution is to spend more time on the problem subject, not less. As you become increasingly familiar with the difficult subject, your skill and confidence will rise, which will improve your overall academic performance. You may even end up liking the subject.

If there are days when you just can't bring yourself to stick to your schedule, don't beat yourself up about it. Simply set aside time the next day, or over the weekend, to make up for the lost studying time, and then stay on track.

CHAPTER 5

DOING YOUR HOMEWORK

Some students view homework as a chore or a punishment. But that's the wrong way to look at it. Doing your homework benefits you in many ways as this chapter will explain.

How Doing Homework Helps You

Homework reinforces what you've been taught, so you can better understand it and remember it. If you didn't do homework, you wouldn't comprehend your subjects nearly as well.

In addition, homework gives you the chance to show your teacher that you're following along with the lessons.

Or if you're actually struggling, your homework can let your teacher know that you need more help.

And most importantly, homework forces you to think and to work in a disciplined way. These are skills that you'll rely upon for the rest of your life, no matter what profession you choose.

The following are some other helpful things about homework:

- **Connects theory to practice:** It's often hard to connect to a subject by just hearing about it or reading about it. It's not until you start performing work on the subject that you start fully understanding it. Homework gives you the chance to turn the theory you learned in class and from your books into practical solutions to problems, which both deepens your understanding and helps you develop great problem-solving skills.

- **Improves your knowledge:** Your teacher assigns you lessons in a thoughtful way to slowly build your understanding of each subject. The more homework you do, the more knowledgeable you'll become, and the better equipped you'll be to succeed later on in your career.

- **Tests your knowledge:** Your homework tests how well you grasped the material covered. You may often find that you didn't fully understand a lesson until you performed the homework for it.

- **Deepens your thinking:** Your homework encourages you to go beyond the surface of any topic and think more deeply about it. Thinking creatively about any topic is a vital skill. If you become skilled at it, it's likely to take you far in your future career.

- **Develops good work habits:** As you grow older, you'll start working for a living. (You might even have a part-time job right now.) Homework helps get you used to working every weekday for set periods of time, researching and absorbing information, and creating something tangible as a result of your learning and thinking. These are all crucial skills for your future career.

- **Helps you know how you're doing:** When you do your homework, you're showing how well you understand the subject that was taught. This is helpful for your teacher, who cares about your progress. But it's also useful to you, because it tells you where you're strong and where you need to spend more time studying.

- **Helps you earn better grades:** The assignments you do for your homework are similar to the tests and quizzes that end up determining your grades. So, the more skilled you become at doing your homework, the more likely you are to perform well academically—and excellent grades can open doors for your future career.

How to Do Your Homework Effectively

The following are tips and tricks that will help you get the most out of the time you spend on school assignments:

- **Make sure you understand the topic:** If you aren't clear about something your teacher says while he or she is explaining a topic, don't hesitate to ask questions. This will save you a lot of time when you're ready to do your homework. It's also great practice for listening carefully and gathering complete information, which are important skills for your future career.

- **Make sure you understand the assignment:** Never make assumptions about what your teacher wants. If you aren't certain about the details of any assignment, don't be shy about asking your teacher questions until you clearly understand what's needed and how you're supposed to perform the homework.

- **Take clear notes:** Take good notes about each subject while your teacher is explaining it, and also take good notes on the details of each assignment. This will save you time when you're ready to perform your homework.

- **Study your notes:** Since you went to the trouble of taking notes, be sure to review them before you start your homework. Your notes may remind you of something important that will save you from mistakes and wasted time. Your notes are also likely to enrich what you write for your homework.

- **Follow instructions:** Once you clearly understand what your teacher wants, stick to his or her wishes. For example, if you're told to explain something in 100 words or less, don't go over 100 words; if you're told to type an assignment, don't write it by hand; and so on.

- **Use your work to grow:** While you should follow instructions, you should also do more than that. Seek to understand why your teacher gave you each assignment and try to get the most out of it. In other words, don't work robotically. Use your homework to enrich your knowledge and your skills, and to grow as a person.

- **Research your topic:** Unless your teacher tells you otherwise, feel encouraged to do research on your subject beyond your assigned reading so you can get a fuller understanding of it. Just keep in mind that not everything on the internet is true, so give the most weight to well-reviewed websites and to well-reviewed books.

- **Don't plagiarize:** It's fine to get information and ideas from your research, but never copy sentences verbatim, because that's stealing the work of someone else. Instead, think about everything you learn in your research, try to come up with whatever original thoughts and insights you can, and then write your results in your own words.

- **Meet deadlines:** When your teacher tells you to hand in an assignment by a certain date, have it ready by that date (if not sooner …). Consistently meeting deadlines is one of the most important habits you can create for yourself. Being able to do this without fail is vital to both your academic performance and to almost any future career.

Finally, as discussed in Chapter 1, don't put your homework off until the last minute. Poet Edward Young wrote, "Procrastination is the thief of time." Start on an assignment early, and give yourself plenty of time to complete it. This will protect you from stress and missed deadlines.

SAMPLE J

Name of Student: **Queen Elizabeth A. Asiedu** Country: **USA** School: **Frederick Douglass Academy V** Class: **Grade 6**

Hobby: **Reading, Dancing And Singing** Career Choice: **Optician**

How to do your homework (sample homework on measurement)

Homework on Measurements

A ——————————————————————————— 15cm

B ————————————————————— 12cm

C ————————————— 8cm

1. Measure A, B and C (in centimeters).
2. Record your answers at the end of the line
3. Compare lines A and B, which one is longer.
4. Line B is longer than line C by how many Centimeters.
5. Add lines A, B and C, what do you get in centimeters.
6. Line A subtract C (line C) from it, what do you get in centimeters.
7. If 100 cm gives you 1 meter. How many meters will you get when you add lines A, B, and C.

I have made a summary of "How to Do Your Homework Effectively," and we are going to use the points in the summary to solve the measurement homework

1. **Read** your homework in detail and plan ahead before putting pen to paper.
2. Pay close attention to the **instructions.**
3. Identify the specific **directions** your teacher gives you in the instructions and follow them.
4. Refer to **your notes** often, especially when in doubt.
5. Use detail **formulas** and **illustrations** where necessary.
6. **Go over your work** at least twice to identify any mistakes when finalizing your work.
7. Make sure to submit your work **before the deadline.** NB: It is always wise to make sure you complete your homework way before the deadline to allow you time to go back and edit if necessary.

Note: Read your measurement homework at least twice or more. In your second or third reading, record or take note of directions and instruction Some of the directions and instructions are

1. **Measure Lines A, B, and C in centimeter**
2. **Answers should be recorded at the end of the line. For the purpose of this sample, I have recorded the answers (in centimeters) on the SAMPLE J image**
3. **Other instruction are to compare, subract, add, relate, and so on**

So, to solve the assignment we have:

1. **When you measure with a ruler, line A - 15cm line, B - 12cm, Line C - 8cm.**
2. **The answers are already recorded at the end of the lines A, B and C (refer to sample J)**
3. **Line A - 15cm, Line B - 12cm. Line A is longer than line B**
4. **Line B - 12cm, Line C- 8cm, 12 - 8 = 4, so Line B is longer than Line C by 4cm**
5. **Adding Lines A, B, and C, that will be 15cm + 12cm + 8cm = 35cm**
6. **Subtracting Line C from Line A, 15cm - 8cm = 7cm**

7. **100cm = 1 meter. Therefore, 35cm will give you 35 x 1 / 100. Solving it will give you 0.35 meters. Note there are several ways of solving this problem.**

Now that your measurement homework is done, submit it on time if it is online. If you have to submit the homework in person, put it in your bag so you don't forget to give it to your teacher when you get to school.

CHAPTER 6

CREATING AND USING A STUDY GUIDE

Another very useful tool is a *study guide*. This is a booklet where you write down the most important points of each of your lessons. By boiling down every class and every textbook chapter to its key takeaways, this booklet makes it a lot easier for you to remember the things you need to know most. It's also an invaluable aid when studying for tests.

You can create and maintain your study guide in a software notepad on your phone or laptop.

Alternatively, you can use a paper notebook. If you go this route, though, make a copy of your notebook's new pages every week. That way if you ever lose the notebook, you'll still have the valuable notes that you worked so hard to create.

Study Guide Examples

The following are some examples of entries you might write in your study guide:

Example 1- Science (Ecology)

- **Organism** - living things
- **Habitat** - A place an organism lives
- **Species** - A group of organisms that produce young ones.
- **Biotic/Abiotic** - Biotic means living, Abiotic means non living
- **Population** - The same organisms live in the same area

- **Community** - Different organisms live in the same area
- **Ecosystem** - A complex of different organisms & their environment

Example 2 English language Arts (Reading Vocabs and Writing tips)

Reading (Vocabulary)
1. Grant — Allow
2. Skill — Ability
3. Compel — Force
4. Humble — Modest
5. Contend — Compete

Writing tips.
1. Read a lot of books etc
2. Do a lot of observation daily
3. Make notes of things around you
4. Try and be imaginative
5. Try and edit your writing

Example 3 Mathematics (Understanding Ratio and Proportions)

Ratio

Oranges   ○   ○   ○

Apples   ♡   ♡   ♡   ♡   ♡

Ratio of oranges to apples is   3:5

Proportion

x	1	2	3	4	5	6
y	2	4	6	8	10	12

x — cups of tea

y — Number of cube sugar

x is then proportional to y

Example 4 History (Presidents, Civil Right and Legislature)

Basic Information in History

1. First president of USA
✓ George Washington

2. Martin Luther King Jr was born
✓ January 15, 1929

3. 2 Major political Parties in the US
✓ Democratic party & Republican party.

4. The U.S. has 2 legislative bodies
✓ House of Representatives & The Senate

5. The senate consist →
✓ 2 Senators from each State
The House of Rep. →
✓ Rep. from congressional Districts

These highlights of lessons are helpful in themselves. They're also memory teasers that remind you of everything else you've learned about the subject.

So look over your class notes and textbooks, pick out the most important parts, and start getting in the habit of entering them into your study guide.

Using Images as Study Aides

Other images that can be helpful range from biology and anatomy diagrams to tables of data and complex scientific formulas.

The more you look at an image, the more details you're likely to notice, and the more you'll probably remember.

It takes time and effort to create an effective study guide. However, that creative process will by itself help you better understand and remember your subjects.

And after you're done, you'll be able to carry around your study guide instead of a dozen textbooks, and easily brush up on any topic when you're studying for a quiz or exam.

Depending on the information you capture, you may find your study guide to be a valuable reference even after you've graduated.

Plus the skills you learn in creating your study guide—that is, taking in lots of information, boiling it down to its most important parts, and clearly and concisely expressing those highlights in a document you can study over and over—are likely to be extremely helpful in whatever career you choose.

Sample of images

Example 6 Science (Revolution of the earth around the sun)

Revolution of the earth around the SUN

Example 7 Math (Shapes)

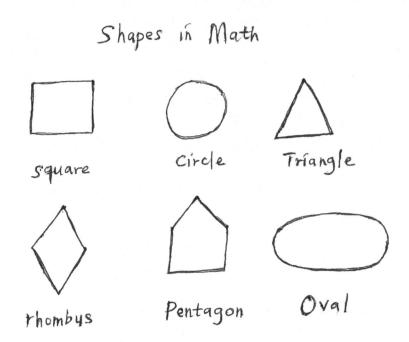

Example 8 Science (The Rock Cycle)

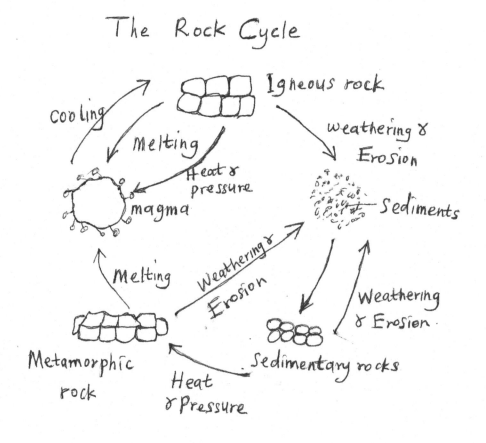

CHAPTER 7

CHOOSING THE RIGHT PLACE TO STUDY

Where you study has a significant impact on how well you study.

For example, if you're trying to read in a living room that has the TV blaring, or in a school cafeteria where your friends come up to say hello every five minutes, you're going to have a hard time concentrating on your work.

In contrast, the following are examples of ideal places to study:

- **Library:** A library is designed to provide you with a calm, quiet environment that's free of distractions so you can focus 100 percent on reading, studying, and doing homework. In addition, a library surrounds you with books and other sources of information in case you need to conduct research beyond your textbooks. You can even ask for help from a librarian—who is a professional researcher—if you have trouble locating a book or other piece of information you need. School libraries, public libraries, and (if you have access to them) university and private libraries are all wonderful places for you to study.

- **Reading room:** Some schools and other institutions have rooms that are devoted to reading and studying. They're more bares-bones than a library, consisting mostly of tables and chairs. However, they typically provide the same calm, quiet, and distraction-free environment. As long as you don't need the research opportunities provided by a library, studying in a reading room is just as good.

- **Nature:** If the weather is pleasant, another wonderful place to study is outside close to nature. For example, if your school has a campus, you could sit under a tree. If you're near a park, you could sit on a park bench surrounded by trees and grass. And if you're near a quiet lake, you could read to the calming sound of water (and maybe the occasional duck). In addition to being free of distractions, the fresh air and sunshine are likely to give you extra energy as you study.

- **Coffee shop:** If you have a laid-back coffee shop, inexpensive diner, or other establishment with chairs and tables in your neighborhood that's quiet and isn't going to rush you out, it might work for you as a kind of study lounge with snacks. If you start engaging in long conversations with the people there, though, then find another spot, because the point is for you to study without distractions.

- **Your room:** If you have a comfortable chair and a good reading lamp, your room can also be an excellent place to study, because it's convenient, cozy, and gives you access to all your books and the Internet in case you need to conduct research. However, your room is effective only if you avoid diversions such as TV and social media during your study hours, and you ask your family to give you privacy every evening until you've completed your work.

If you find yourself frequently distracted in your room, though, or if instead of working you end up eating and/or falling asleep, then consider studying somewhere that forces you to focus instead.

Everyone has their own individual needs, so the bottom line is to do whatever works best for you. For example, certain students thrive in libraries, others do better outdoors, and others are more productive in their rooms. If you're not sure which environment is the best fit for you, experiment by working in different places and seeing how much you get accomplished in each setting.

Also keep in mind that people in the past have managed to not only read books but write their own books under highly challenging conditions, such as while battling in a war zone or being imprisoned. What matters even more than your workspace is your desire and determination to succeed.

That said, if being in a library is going to make studying easier for you and you have the opportunity to go to that library, then why not do that? Creating the conditions that help you do your best work is one of the most important skills you can develop, both as a student and in your future career.

CHAPTER 8

TAKING CARE OF YOURSELF

You can achieve your academic and professional goals only if you're healthy. While studying is important, so is taking excellent care of yourself.

There are a number of hazards that can threaten you in high school. Among the most common are bad eating habits, accidents, crime, alcohol and other drugs, emotional issues, and unplanned and unwanted consequences of sex. Each of these will be briefly touched upon in this chapter. If you're dealing with one of these problems, though, don't hesitate to ask for help from your parents, a school counselor, a youth center, a local religious leader, and/or other adults you trust. Don't try to deal with a serious situation on your own. Instead, reach out to the many resources available to you and the many people who want to help you.

The statistics in this chapter refer to students in the U.S. However, the trends they represent are generally true in all countries.

Eat Well

Food might not sound like a significant danger to your health. But if you consistently eat the wrong things, you may damage your ability to concentrate and study well. And down the line, you may develop serious diseases that you could have otherwise avoided.

It's tempting to eat inexpensive burgers, pizza, and snacks every day. But foods that are cheap, and consist mostly of fat and/or sugar, aren't good for you.

It's much healthier to skip processed foods and get in the habit of eating fresh vegetables and fruits. And it's even better if you eat organic produce. A diet that consists mostly of organic fruits and veggies is likely to give you a clear mind, a body that can stay active longer, and way fewer sick days that slow you down.

For detailed advice about eating well:

Visit the U.S. Office of Disease Prevention and Health Promotion website at Health.gov/dietary guidelines.

Avoid Accidents

It may shock you to learn that by far the biggest danger for students aged twelve to nineteen, accounting for nearly 50 percent of teen deaths, is *accidents*. And about 75 percent of those accidents are the result of motor vehicle crashes.

As a result, be picky about whose car you enter. If a driver appears intoxicated or reckless, or gives you any other reason to feel uncomfortable, bow out and get another ride.

And even when you do trust a driver, always wear a seat belt.

Alternatively, if you're driving yourself, keep these tips in mind:

- Always scan the roadway and check mirrors. You should always be aware of what vehicles and potential obstacles are nearby.
- Don't drive too fast for the conditions of your road. That's especially true when it's raining, snowing, or dark. (And, needless to say, don't exceed the speed limit.)
- If you're still learning to drive, don't drive at night. Many fatal teen crashes happen between 9:00 p.m. and midnight, not because of recklessness but simple inexperience. Until you've mastered driving, stick to daylight hours.
- Always wear a seat belt, and make each of your passengers wear a seat belt.
- Never drink and drive.
- Never do drugs and drive.
- Never text and drive.
- Don't drive with friends piled into your car, as that vastly increases the chances of an accident happening. Limit passengers to one to three friends.
- Don't let anything distract you from the road, such as loud music, your passengers, or something that's happening outside of your car. Stay alert and focused.
- Always keep your eyes on the road and your hands on the wheel. Nothing is more important than driving safely.

More generally, avoid accidents by always being aware of what's going on around you, anticipating what can potentially go wrong, and having plans for dealing with whatever might happen.

Avoid Alcohol and Other Drugs

While motor vehicle accidents are the biggest cause of teen deaths, that's not the whole story. About 50 percent of those accidents happen because of a teen drinking alcohol and then driving.

- And beyond fatalities, over 250,000 students aged fifteen to twenty are injured every year in motor vehicle crashes, frequently as a result of drinking.
- Alcohol is also the leading cause of students attacking other students, students becoming the victims of attack or rape, and students getting arrested.
- And if all that wasn't awful enough, more than 150,000 students a year develop an alcohol-related health problem.
- It's illegal to buy alcohol in the US if you're under age twenty-one. And the statistics just mentioned are the reasons why.

Obey the law, and don't drink alcohol until you're truly ready for it.

Along the same lines, avoid all other addictive drugs. Opioids, heroin, cocaine, and other such substances are highly dangerous. While alcohol can encourage behavior that leads to death or injury, other drugs—and especially opioids—can kill their users outright. In fact, over 70,000 Americans a year die of overdoses, and around 5,000 of them are teens.

Treat your body as a temple. Don't pollute it with substances that are bad for you.

To learn more about alcohol and drug abuse, visit these sites:

1. National Institute on Drug Abuse (**DrugAbuse.gov**): This US federal agency provides in-depth information on the health effects of specific drugs.
2. Substance Abuse and Mental Health Services Administration (**SAMHSA. gov**): This U.S. federal agency provides a drug treatment center locator that you can use to confidentially find local help.
3. National Clearinghouse for Alcohol & Drug Information (**Health.org**): Hosts numerous articles, news stories, and studies about drugs.
4. Monitoring the Future (**MonitoringTheFuture.org**): Provides in-depth national studies of high school student behavior and attitudes toward drugs.

Keep Safe

Sadly, 13 percent of teen deaths in the U.S. result from homicide. And most of those are gun-related.

While you shouldn't live in fear, you shouldn't be blindly trusting either. Those aged fifteen to twenty-five are among the most likely to both commit and be victimized by crime.

Here are some tips for remaining safe:

1. If possible, walk with a companion at night.
2. Avoid poorly lit or isolated areas, and unsafe neighborhoods.
3. Avoid a group of strangers, especially if they appear intoxicated.
4. Don't let strangers into your building.
5. Don't get into an elevator with anyone who makes you uncomfortable.
6. If threatened, blow a whistle if you have one.
7. If threatened, call 911 ASAP to ensure your safety.

Maintain Your Mental Health

While you wouldn't hesitate to see a doctor if you fractured your ankle or got an infection, many teens resist seeking help when something goes wrong with their mental health.

That's because there's an irrational stigma attached to depression, anxiety, OCD, and other common mental issues.

This is a tragedy, because the latter can be at least as disruptive and painful to young lives. For example, 11 percent of teen deaths result from suicide, primarily stemming from clinical depression.

The truth is that some of the famous and successful people of our time have suffered from depression, including **Harrison Ford, Brad Pitt, Lady Gaga, Angelina Jolie, Johnny Depp, Dolly Parton, Jim Carrey, Demi Lovato, Gwyneth Paltrow, Jon Hamm, Ellen Degeneres, Kristen Bell, Eminem, Britney Spears, Reese Witherspoon, and J.K. Rowling**. Each of them reached out for help; and each of them eventually got better and proceeded to conquer the world.

If you're struggling with any kind of mental or emotional issue, don't suffer in silence. Tell your parents, and get help from a psychiatrist, psychologist, therapist, or another professional who's trained to treat mental issues.

Also try being extra picky about what you put in your body (see the previous "Eat Well" and "Avoid Alcohol and Other Drugs" sections). If you cut out processed foods and anything else that's bad for you and make a habit of eating mostly fresh vegetables and fruits—including a daily cup of blueberries or wild blueberries, which are exceptionally high in antioxidants—over a few months your body and brain chemistry will probably start changing, and that alone might make you feel better.

Here are resources worth exploring for help and further information:

1. Suicide Hotlines ((800) SUICIDE/(800) 784-2433; **suicidehotlines.com**): If you're thinking about harming yourself, or know someone else who is, pick up a phone and call this service, which has people ready to speak with you 24/7. They'll put you in touch with a suicide hotline in your area that can provide additional support.
2. National Alliance for the Mentally Ill (**nami.org**): This nonprofit organization maintains a free Helpline at (800) 950-6264 to find a NAMI affiliate office near you, which in turn can refer you to a professional trained to treat you.
3. Depression & Bipolar Support Alliance (**dbsalliance.org**): This nonprofit organization hosts both in-person and online support groups. Visit the site or call (800) 826-3632 to find groups in your area.

National Institute of Mental Health (**nimh.nih.gov**): This U.S. federal site hosts lots of information about mental illness, including publications about depression at **nimh.nih.gov/publicat/depression.cfm.**

Be Thoughtful About Sex

When you become a teen, you also start to become a sexual being. But just because your body suddenly becomes capable of having sex doesn't mean you're ready for it. Often the best way to handle sex is with patience. Wait until you are emotionally matured to have sex, or better still for when you get married. Abstinence is the best advice I can give you as a junior high school student.

Some teens say, "Well, we can use condoms to protect ourselves," but this is not necessarily the truth. Many people who have tried this have themselves with some of the biggest physical hazards of sex, including contracting sexually transmitted diseases (STDs), accidental pregnancy and so on.

If you need help or any advice on how to stay away from sex, contact any certified counsellor of your school with a clean record and background check. Also, you can get help from your local community clinic, hospital or designated health facility. As a young student the best people to ask for help are your parents. Gather the courage and talk to them for help before it's too late.

CHAPTER 9

BECOMING WHO YOU'RE MEANT TO BE

School has many purposes. It helps you learn about the world, teaches you to think, and encourages you to be disciplined about your work.

But another major purpose of school is to prepare you for eventually leaving it and pursuing your career.

If you believe—as I do—that things happen for a reason, then it follows everyone on earth has a purpose. No one is here by chance. Each of us was born to achieve something and make an impact.

Along the same lines, each of us has at least one talent that can be the foundation of an exciting career. A way of identifying that talent is to notice what interests you. Whatever field draws you in the most powerfully may be the field you were born to pursue.

This is important, because when you have a career that you love and is perfectly suited for you, you're able to leverage your complete potential, do your very best work, and feel entirely fulfilled. And when that happens, you're likely to achieve success and happiness.

Further, when you're at the best, you're helping everyone on Earth who benefits, directly or indirectly, from your excellent work. In other words, when you're in a career that lets your true self shine, the world is a better place for it.

Conversely, if you fail to discover or pursue your calling and instead settle for a life that's inauthentic, you suffer from it, and so does everyone whose lives would've been enriched from your working at your best.

For both your sake and the sake of everyone who will in some way be affected by you, you should do all you can to choose the career that's meant for you.

There are a number of books to help you with this journey. They include the following:

- *What Color Is Your Parachute? for Teens,* by Carol Christen
- *What Color Is Your Parachute?*, by Richard N. Bolles
- *The Pathfinder: How to Choose or Change Your Career*, by Nicholas Lore
- *Do What You Are*, by Paul D. Tieger, Kelly Tieger, and Barbara Barron
- *What is Your WHAT?*, by Steve Olsher (free at WhatIsYourWhat.com)

Clues to Your Career

No one is born with a sign attached to their forehead saying, "When I grow up, I'm going to be a **doctor**" or, "I'm going to be a **computer programmer**" or, "I'm going to be a **dancer**." But if you listen carefully to your feelings, you may pick up some clues to your destiny.

For example, do you have a strong desire to help people with their troubles? Does your heart go out to those in pain or difficulty? This can indicate a career in service, ranging from **medicine** to **social work** to **politics**.

Do you love working with the land and nature? This can lead to becoming a **farmer**, or a **park ranger**, or a **botanist**.

Does it fill you with joy to dream up ideas and put them together creatively? This can forge a path for work as a **writer,** or an **attorney**, or a **physicist**.

Notice where your passions take you. If you have a strong inner drive that keeps you going towards something, no matter what obstacles are placed in your way, then you might be happy pursuing that goal professionally.

Also worth considering are your natural strengths.

- Are you a persuasive speaker?
- Are you unusually kind?
- Are you a bold leader?
- Are you exceptionally persistent?
- Are you powerfully athletic?
- Do you have a great ear for music?

- Do you make people laugh?

Any of these gifts, or any combination of them, can help guide you to a particular career.

You may encounter people who try to discourage you from your chosen path. If they make good points, listen to them. But if they don't, then start surrounding yourself with people who cheer you on for following your dreams—and who may even have the same career goals. They might become part of a lifelong support network for you.

Most of all, listen to your heart, your gut, and your own intellect. This is especially true if you've chosen a difficult profession. Don't give up just because people tell you it'll be hard. If you're honest with yourself about your talents and your drive to succeed in a particular career, then stay focused and honor your instincts.

If you're ever in doubt, let love and your desire to help others guide you.

President John F. Kennedy said, "Ask not what your country can do for you. Ask what you can do for your country."

So, if your faith in yourself ever falters, hold onto your determination to serve others with your gifts.

Get to Know Your Chosen Field

Once you choose a career, don't wait until you graduate to pursue it. Start right away.

First, learn more about it. Read or listen to books, watch videos, talk to people already in the field, and absorb as much as you can.

Second, if possible, get an internship. For example, if you're interested in journalism, apply to help out at a newspaper, magazine, or news broadcast station. If you're interested in finance, apply for an internship at a bank or an equity trading desk. If you're interested in medicine, apply for an internship at a hospital or medical research firm. And so on.

You typically won't be paid for your time, but you'll have the opportunity to soak in invaluable real-world information and experience about your chosen profession. Further, you'll have the chance to meet and impress people who are in a position to later recommend you to employers—or even hire you themselves.

If you fully leverage your internship with such practices, it can be a way to get ahead of students who spend time exclusively on their schoolwork.

Then again, if you've chosen a career for which an internship isn't meaningful—for example, writing books, making music, or doing stand-up comedy—then instead of interning, start actually doing it. If you want to be a book author, develop the habit of writing every day. If you want to create music or deliver stand-up, work hard on your material daily, and perform regularly in front of audiences. Doing so will give you a sense of whether this is really the right career for you. Plus, the most important way to get better in fields such as the arts is to keep at it, day after day, until you become truly great at it.

Seek Role Models and Mentors

I was once in a classroom where a teacher went around asking each of the students what career he or she wanted.

One boy replied, "A lawyer."

"Why?" asked the teacher.

"Because my dad is one," said the boy.

"How are you going to become a lawyer?" the teacher asked.

Without hesitating, the boy answered, "By watching my dad and following in his footsteps."

Among the most helpful things you can do for your future career is find role models whose examples you can follow. Their success is proof that your dreams are achievable, and their own careers can inspire you.

In addition, find one or more *mentors*. A mentor is someone who's already done what you want to do professionally and is willing to use his or her many years of experience to advise and guide you.

In the story just mentioned, the boy who wanted to be a lawyer had his father available to be a mentor. But there are many ways to find a mentor: through relatives, friends, school contacts, business contacts, and more.

For example, one of the reasons to get an internship in your chosen field is that it puts you in frequent contact with people who, if they're impressed by you, can decide to help you, mentor you, and even hire you.

So, as you start interacting with people in your chosen field, always keep an eye out for potential mentors.

On a related note, try to develop excellent relationships with the teachers you most admire. They can write you recommendations for your internship applications and college applications. And they can sometimes also put you in touch with professionals in your desired career who end up as your mentors and/or employers.

Be Open to Change

Part of the point of both high school and college is to give you exposure to a wide range of fields. The hope is that you'll find something that resonates for you and that you recognize as your calling.

As a result, sometimes the career you think you want for practical reasons—e.g., you believe it'll earn you a lot of money, or it's what your parents want you to do—is abruptly jettisoned when you run across a profession for which you feel a shockingly powerful connection and for which you have a natural gift. In the long run, feeling passionate about work that you have the innate talent to excel at is one of the best ways to ensure you give 100 percent to your career and become exceptionally successful at it.

At the same time, jobs don't happen in a vacuum. We live in the most rapidly changing global conditions in history. You must also pay attention to what's happening in the world to ensure a career you're leaning toward will even exist in five years, as opposed to being replaced or radically altered as a result of artificial intelligence technology or other advances.

Therefore, be open to making changes to your initial plans. Take full advantage of the opportunities provided by your time as a student to explore different fields; also keep an eye on what's happening in business, science, technology, and political news; carefully consider all your possibilities, and then choose a career that's truly the best fit for you.

CHAPTER 10

YES, YOU CAN

Believe in yourself, put into practice what you have read in this book, do your best, and you'll succeed.

You'll also make an impact on your generation and generations to come.

Whenever you're in doubt, just remember to say to yourself, "Yes, I can!"

And then go prove it.

ACKNOWLEDGEMENTS

Special thanks to Lord God Almighty, for the wisdom given to me to come up with such a great idea to help our students.

I say a big thank you to my very good friend **Professor Gene Adams** (Director of Bronx Community College Educative Program and Co-Director of Science and Technology Entry Program) who gave me a foreword for *Yes I Can—Your Guide to Junior High School Academic Success*. Thank you for your leadership and mentorship over the years.

I am deeply grateful to the following people, whose time, talents, and ideas contributed to this book: My wife, Mrs. **Ama Kyere Kesewa**, for being by my side in both the good times and difficult ones. My parents, **Anthony Kwaku Kyere** and **Agnes Abena Kyere**, for their care, love and support. My brothers, **Evans Nyarko Kyere**, **Dr. Vincent Nartey Kyere (PhD)**, and **Emmanuel Asenso Kyere** for their unflinching love and help in realizing my dreams.

I am also very grateful to these servants of God who, despite residing in Ghana, have supported me spiritually and made a great contribution to this book. To **Overseer Jonathan Obeng** (General Overseer of the Jehovah Rapha Prayer Ministry International–Suhum, E/R Ghana), **Prophetess Elizabeth Okrah Obeng** (Founder of Jehovah Rapha Prayer Ministry International) in Ghana, **Apostle Sydney Quaye**, and **Mrs Renny Ose Barima Quaye** (Shekinah Avenue Church–Accra Ghana). Lastly, to **Prophet Philip Kwadwo Boadi,** and his wife **Mrs. Christiana Boadi,** leader and founder of House of Prayer Evangelistic Ministry in Kumasi for supporting me in this endeavor.

Thanks to these servants of God in New York (USA): **Rev. and Mrs. Chika Nndari**-(Covenant Elevation Christian Center), **Rev. and Mrs. Sheriff Rabbonni** (Christ Centered Ministry), **Rev. Felicia Sarpong Gambrah** (New Glory Prayer Fellowship) for their encouragement.

David S. Kyere

Special thanks to **Malcolm Sowah,** who helped me to prepare the manuscript, connected me to Authorhouse and did all the administrative work on my behalf. Malcolm has been a tremendous help in getting this book published.

I am very grateful to **Mr. Arda Beskardes**, attorney-at-law in Brooklyn, New York, for assisting me in all my legal and paper works.

I want to thank Mr. **Hy Bender**, a writing coach, who helped me in organizing the manuscript into a perfect order.

To all the **AuthorHouse team**, who helped to design, typeset, and publish the book. Thank you for your time and such great and excellent work.

I also want to thank **PS 109** (Elementary School in the Bronx), **Principal Josette Claudio,** Assistant Principal **Diana Castillo**, and Assistant Principal **Yoli-Ann Barrett** for giving me the opportunity to serve as a substitute teacher at the time I was writing this book. I thank the wonderful staff, the teachers, and all the workers for their support. I thank **Mrs. Stephanie Romero,** an excellent and hardworking teacher in whose class I spent more time and gained a lot of experience.

I am very grateful to **Barbara Shut**, an educational consultant, and **John De Angelis**, a stewart in the publishing industry, for their guidance and direction in putting the manuscript together.

Finally, I cannot forget to thank all our **junior high school students** who volunteered to do and share their personal timetable in this book. To all **the parents** who gave permission to their children to support me in this endeavor, I say thank you.

THE AUTHOR

Apostle David S. Kyere attended the Seventh Day Adventist Junior High School and graduated at the Pope John Senior High school in Ghana, West Africa. Mr. Kyere then received his bachelor's degree at the Kwame Nkrumah University Science and Technology in Renewable Natural Resources Management in Kumasi, Ghana.

At the University of California–Riverside, Apostle David Kyere completed his post graduate work in Global Business Management and Administration and moved on to New Life Bible College in Virginia to complete his master's degree in Christian Ministry, USA. Apostle David is currently at City College of New York, completing his Master of Arts degree in Secondary Science Education.

Mr. Kyere is also the founder of the Jehovah Rapha Fellowship, a student organization in Ghana which has helped lots of students attain academic success and overcome all kinds of addictions. As a co-director of Jehovah Rapha foundation, Mr. Kyere partnered with World Vision and United States Agency for International Development (USAID) to provide basic resources, such as food and education, to orphans and vulnerable children.

Currently, Apostle David S. Kyere is the resident pastor of Jehovah Rapha Prayer Ministry International, a predominantly youth church in the Bronx, where he mentors students on spiritual growth and academic success.

Mr. Kyere also authored **The New York State-approved textbook on academic intervention,** *YES I CAN—Guidelines for Studies for High School Students.*

Mr. Kyere has worked with many children, students, and educators over the years. His passion has always been to teach and create academic intervention programs and workshops to help students overcome various barriers and become successful.

ABOUT THE BOOK

Yes, I Can—Your Guide to Junior High School Academic Success is designed to help junior high school students strengthen their academic, career, and life goals. This special book offers students strategies for improving their study skills, time management, and career planning.

Yes, I Can—Your Guide to Junior High School Academic Success uniquely explains how students can manage their time, study effectively and efficiently, practice excellent selfcare, and find their true selves. By building their skills and confidence, it will help students balance their academic work with their personal lives and do their very best academically. It will also guide students and young individuals to develop good habits for a highly successful future career.

After reading this book, students will be able to confidently take charge of their academic and personal success.

Printed in the United States
by Baker & Taylor Publisher Services